RAILWAYS OF
EAST SUSSEX

1948–1968

Peter Waller

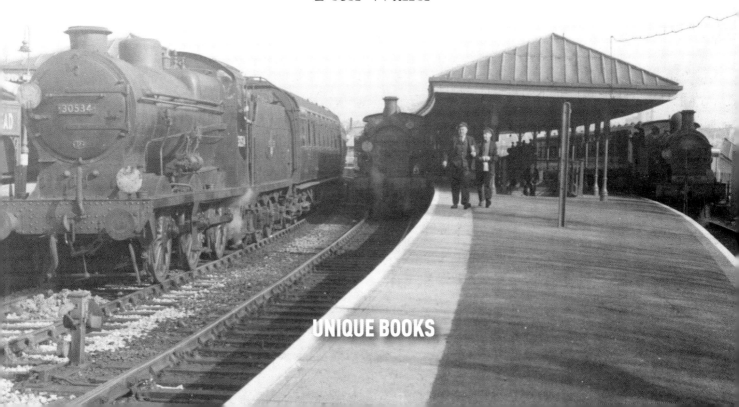

UNIQUE BOOKS

Front cover:
On 7 May 1955 BR Standard 2-6-4T No 80033 stands in East Grinstead station with a southbound service towards Lewes.
Neil Davenport/Online Transport Arch

Previous page:
A busy scene at East Grinstead High Level station on 15 March 1958 sees Class Q No 30534 on a westbound passenger service alongside two unidentified Class H 0-4-4Ts. Designed by Richard Maunsell, the first of the 'Q' class emerged from Eastleigh Works in 1938 under Maunsell's successor as Chief Mechanical Engineer. A total of 20 were constructed during 1938 and 1939. The class was primarily designed to replace small older locomotives with a high route availability for freight and light passenger duties. Between 1940 and 1947 all 20 were rebuilt – as seen here – with Lemaître blast pipes and chimneys with seven undergoing a further modification – utilising a BR Standard blastpipe and small stovepipe chimney – between 1955 and 1961. All were withdrawn between 1962 and 1965 with No 30541 eventually being preserved, having been originally sold for scrap to the Woodham Bros scrapyard at Barry. No 30451 is now based on the Bluebell Railway. *John Meredith/Online Transport Archive*

Railways of East Sussex: 1948–1968
Peter Waller

First published in the United Kingdom by Unique Books 2022

ISBN: 978 1 913555 09 2

Unique Books is an imprint of Unique Publishing Services Ltd, 3 Merton Court, The Strand, Brighton Marina Village, Brighton BN2 5XY.

www.uniquebooks.pub

Printed in India

A note on the photographs
Most of the illustrations in this book have been drawn from the collection of the Online Transport Archive, a UK-registered charity that was set up to accommodate collections put together by transport enthusiasts who wished to see their precious images secured for the long-term. Further information about the archive can be found at:
www.onlinetransportarchive.org
or email secretary@onlinetransportarchive.org

INTRODUCTION

The development of the railways of East Sussex was dominated by two pre-Grouping companies: the London, Brighton & South Coast and the South Eastern (later the South Eastern & Chatham) railways. The two were brought into common ownership at the Grouping in 1923 as the Southern Railway. This became the Southern Region of British Railways at Nationalisation in January 1948. Even under SR and BR ownership, there remained a distinction: the ex-LBSCR lines effectively formed the South Central whilst the ex-SECR South Eastern. This split persisted through much of the BR period and largely only disappeared when the railways were sectorised in the 1980s with all the surviving passenger lines in the area becoming part of Network SouthEast.

The first railway in the district was the London & Brighton; this was authorised by an Act of 15 July 1837 to construct a line from the planned London & Croydon through to Brighton. Although the line from Brighton westwards to Shoreham was the first of the company's authorised routes to open, the main line opened from Norwood to Haywards Heath on 12 July 1841 and thence to Brighton on 21 September 1841. Following several amalgamations, the company's name was changed to the London, Brighton & South Coast Railway in 1946. Services on the London to Brighton main line were electrified from 1 January 1933.

The line from Brighton to Hastings was promoted by the Brighton, Lewes & Hastings Railway, which was absorbed by the London & Brighton whilst under construction. The line opened in stages: from Brighton to Lewes on 8 June 1846, thence to Bulverhythe on 27 June 1846, to St Leonards on 7 November 1846 and finally to Hastings – where a joint station with the SER was established – on 13 January 1851. The line was electrified by the SR from 7 July 1935. The cut-off route from Wivelsfield to Lewes was also authorised to the Brighton, Lewes & Hastings Railway in 1845 but ownership had passed to the LBSCR by the time that the line opened on 1 October 1847.

Promoted by the LBSCR, which saw in Newhaven a harbour that could be developed for the growing cross-Channel traffic, the line from Lewes to Newhaven (known as Newhaven Town from 1864) opened on 8 December 1847 along with an extension into the harbour that served Newhaven Wharf. The line was extended through to Seaford on 1 June 1864. Newhaven Wharf station became Newhaven Harbour station in 1884 but the terminal platforms were closed with the opening of Newhaven East Quay (which had various names until finally becoming Newhaven Marine on 14 May 1984; it was closed in August 2006 although timetabled services had ceased earlier) leaving the through platforms on the Seaford branch open. The line from Brighton to Seaford via Lewes was electrified from 7 July 1935.

The LBSCR branch from Polegate to Eastbourne opened on 14 May 1849; the line was originally single track but was subsequently doubled as traffic to the increasingly popular resort grew. The station was rebuilt in 1866, slightly resited in 1872 and again rebuilt in 1886, when the current station was constructed to the design of F. D. Brick. The line from Wivelsfield via Lewes to Eastbourne was also electrified by the SR on 7 July 1935.

The SER line from Tonbridge was extended to the permanent Tunbridge Wells (later Central) station on 25 November 1846 but proposals for the extension of the line southwards to Hastings were delayed as a result of the government's desire that completion of the line from Ashford to Hastings, which was deemed to have a strategic importance, was prioritised. It was not, therefore, until 1 September 1851 that the line opened from Tunbridge Wells to Robertsbridge. The line was extended from Robertsbridge to Battle on 1 January 1851 and thence to Bopeep Junction, on the line from Eastbourne to Hastings, on 1 February 1852. Almost immediately after the line's completion problems started to emerge as a result of the poor quality of the workmanship in the tunnels following the partial collapse of the brickwork in Mountfield Tunnel in March 1855. The remedial work resulted in additional brick lining being required in the tunnels; one consequence of this was that the loading gauge along the route was restricted, requiring the operation of special rolling stock. Problems with the tunnels have persisted for more than a century with the track now singled through a number of them, most notably at Wadhurst and Mountfield. Although proposals for the route's electrification were made earlier, it was not until 27 April 1986 that electric services commenced. One consequence of the singling in certain tunnels is that the line is now the usual loading gauge.

Both the Brighton, Lewes & Hastings and the South Eastern railways had aspirations to construct a line linking Ashford with Hastings; in the event it was the latter that obtained the powers to construct the line. The line finally opened throughout on 13 February 1851. Apart from the short section from Hastings to Ore – which was electrified as part of the expansion of the SR network launched on 7 July 1935 – the Ashford to Hastings line remains diesel operated. The section from Ore to Ashford was proposed for closure in the Beeching

Report but the line was reprieved largely as a result of the problems in providing suitable alternative public transport; the associated branch line to New Romney, in Kent, was not so lucky, closing on 6 March 1967.

The East Grinstead Railway from Three Bridges to East Grinstead was authorised by an Act of 8 July 1853 and opened on 9 July 1855; the line thence to Tunbridge Wells was authorised, courtesy of the East Grinstead, Groombridge & Tunbridge Wells Railway, on 7 August 1862 and opened on 1 October 1866. Listed for closure as part of the Beeching Report, the line closed between Three Bridges and Groombridge on 2 January 1967; however, it was not until 8 July 1985 that the line from Eridge to Tunbridge Wells Central succumbed. The section from Eridge to Tunbridge Wells West was preserved and now operates as the Spa Valley Railway.

The first stage of the link between Lewes and Tunbridge Wells came with the Lewes & Uckfield Railway; this was authorised by an Act of 27 July 1857 and line opened officially on 11 October 1858. Worked by the LBSCR from opening, the line was formally absorbed by the larger railway on 31 May 1860. The line into Lewes itself was realigned on 1 October 1868. The line from Uckfield to Groombridge via Eridge was authorised as the Brighton, Uckfield & Tunbridge Wells Railway by an Act of 22 July 1861. Acquired by the LBSCR prior to opening, the completed line was opened throughout to freight traffic in 1867 and to passenger services on 3 August 1868. Scheduled for closure in the Beeching Report, buses replaced trains south of Uckfield on 24 February 1969 with the official date of closure being 6 May 1969. The section through to Uckfield remained open, although the station at Uckfield was relocated slightly to the north on 13 May 1991. The station at Isfield and one mile of track now form the preserved Lavender Line.

The Lewes & East Grinstead Railway was authorised

by an Act of 10 August 1877 and included the line linking Lewes with East Grinstead as well as the branch from Horsted Keynes to Copyhold Junction north of Haywards Heath. Problems raising the finance for the line led to a further Act the following year that permitted the LBSCR to back the new railway. The line between East Grinstead and Lewes opened on 1 August 1882 with the section from Horsted Keynes to Copyhold Junction following on 3 September 1883. The line from Copyhold Junction to Horsted Keynes was electrified as part of the SR's modernisation during the 1930s with services commencing on 7 July 1935. Passenger services were to have been withdrawn between East Grinstead and Lewes on 13 June 1955 but industrial action resulted in a premature cessation on 28 May 1955. However, investigation into the original Acts resulted in legal action with the result that limited services were restored on 7 August 1956 whilst BR sought the powers formally to close the line. With these obtained, passenger services were again withdrawn on 17 March 1958. The section from Sheffield Park to Horsted Keynes was, however, preserved as the Bluebell Railway and the line has been progressively reopened from Horsted Keynes to East Grinstead. Although electrified, the line from Copyhold Junction to Haywards Heath was already under threat of closure at the time of the Beeching Report and passenger services ceased on 28 October 1963. The section from Copyhold Junction to Ardingly, however, remained open for stone traffic. The trackbed east of Ardingly is owned by the Bluebell Railway, which has a long-term aspiration to rebuild the section and reopen the line through to Haywards Heath.

The origins of the line linking Polegate with Eridge – which became known as the Cuckoo Line – was the branch from Polegate to Hailsham that was authorised in 1846 and opened by the LBSCR on 14 May 1849. The initial proposal by the Tunbridge Wells &

Eastbourne Railway was for the construction of a 3ft 0in gauge line between Hailsham and Eridge; when this struggled to raise the necessary finance, the LBSCR took over following an Act of 27 June 1876 to construct a standard gauge line. It opened from Hailsham to Heathfield on 5 April 1880 and thence to Eridge on 1 September 1880. The junction at Polegate was altered in 1881 so that trains approached the station from the west rather than the east, thus permitting services to operate into Eastbourne without reversing. The Cuckoo Line was one of those listed for closure in the Beeching Report of March 1963 and passenger services were withdrawn between Hailsham and Eridge on 14 June 1965 (at the same time the section between Heathfield and Eridge was closed completely); the surviving services on the section from Hailsham to Polegate were withdrawn on 8 September 1968. Freight traffic continued on the section between Polegate and Heathfield until 26 April 1968 when they cut back to Hailsham. Freight facilities were withdrawn from Hailsham on 5 August 1968 and so the withdrawal of the remaining passenger services the following month saw the final closure of the route.

The section of line north from Ashurst Junction to Hurst Green was the LBSCR-backed Oxted & Groombridge Railway, which was authorised by an Act of 11 August 1881 and opened from Hurst Green Junction to Edenbridge on 2 January 1888 and thence to Ashurst Junction on 1 October 1888.

There was only one line in the area that was not eventually part of either the LBSCR or SER; this was the Rother Valley Railway. Authorised on 2 July 1896 following the Light Railways Act of earlier that year, the 12-mile line opened from Robertsbridge to Tenterden (late renamed Rolvenden when the line was extended northwards) officially on 26 March 1900 and to the public on 2 April 1900. The line was extended to

Tenterden on 16 March 1903 and, following approval of the extension to Headcorn, the company's name was changed to the Kent & East Sussex Railway on 1 June 1904. The Tenterden to Headcorn section opened on 15 May 1905. Passenger services ceased over the entire line on 4 January 1954; the section north from Tenterden Town closed completely at the same time. Freight traffic to Tenterden Town ceased on 12 June 1961 leaving the short section from Robertsbridge to Hodson's Siding operational; this section closed on 1 January 1970. The preserved Kent & East Sussex Railway has progressively reopened the line south from Tenterden Town to the site of Junction Road Halt whilst a second scheme, based at Robertsbridge, has started to reconstruct the line eastwards. At the time of writing a decision as to whether to permit the two sections to be reunited is awaited.

Backed by the SER and operated by it from opening, the Crowhurst, Sidley & Bexhill Railway was authorised by an Act of 15 July 1897 and opened throughout on 1 June 1902; this was the last main line railway to be completed in East Sussex. It was formally absorbed by the SER on 1 January 1907. Scheduled for closure in the Beeching Report, passenger services were withdrawn on 15 June 1964.

1 SALEHURST HALT
2 JUNCTION ROAD
3 SIDLEY
4 BEXHILL WEST
5 ST LEONARDS WARRIOR SQUARE
6 WEST ST LEONARDS
7 ST LEONARDS (WEST MARINA)
8 GLYNE GAP HALT
9 BEXHILL CENTRAL
10 COLLINGTON
11 COODEN BEACH
12 NORMANS BAY
13 PEVENSEY BAY
14 STONE CROSS HALT
15 POLEGATE
16 MAYFIELD
17 ROTHERFIELD & MARK CROSS
18 TUNBRIDGE WELLS WEST
19 HIGH ROCKS HALT
20 GROOMBRIDGE
21 WITHYHAM
22 HARTFIELD
23 FOREST ROW
24 GRANGE ROAD
25 ROWFANT
26 ARDINGLY
27 KINGSCOTE
28 NEWICK & CHAILEY
29 PLUMPTON
30 COOKSBRIDGE
31 BERWICK
32 FALMER
33 MOULSCOOMB
34 LONDON ROAD (BRIGHTON)
35 KEMP TOWN

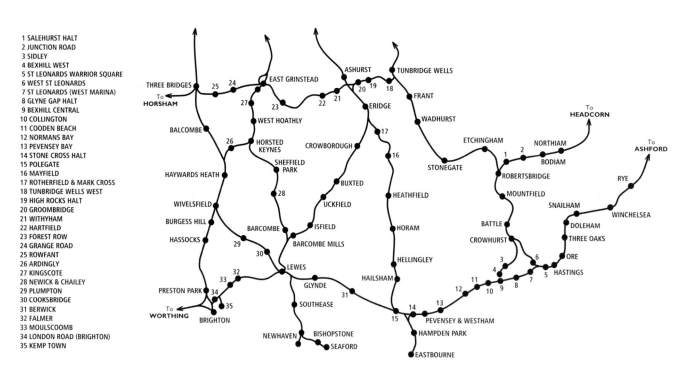

As Type 3 (later Class 33) No D65761 heads northwards on the front of an engineering train, DEMU No 1301 strands in the bay platform awaiting departure with a service towards East Grinstead and Tunbridge Wells on 1 January 1967 – the last day on which passenger services operated over this ex-LBSCR branch. Authorised as the East Grinstead Railway in 1853 the branch opened on 9 July 1855; it was extended through to Tunbridge Wells seven years later. The 19-strong Class 3D (later Class 207) 'East Sussex' units were constructed at Eastleigh Works and introduced in 1962 with narrower bodies to permit operation through the restricted tunnels in the Tunbridge Wells area. Allocated to St Leonards for maintenance purposes, the type was generally based at Tunbridge Wells West. With the closure of the lines from Three Bridges to Tunbridge Wells and from Eridge to Polegate, the type saw operation more widely. A number were withdrawn in 1987 following the electrification of the line to East Grinstead; the last survivors soldiered on into the first years of the 21st century. No 1301 was withdrawn in April 1994 and subsequently scrapped.
John Meredith/Online Transport Archive

On 7 October 1962 two Class 6PUL units, with No 3011 leading, form the 11.25am service from Victoria to Littlehampton as it enters Balcombe station. The 20 '6PUL' units, originally Nos 2001-20 (and later Nos 3001-20), were introduced in 1932 to provide improved accommodation on the line between Brighton and London, which had been recently electrified, and each set included a single Pullman coach; there were an additional three sets – originally Nos 2041-43 (later Nos 3041-43) – that were designated '6CIT' for use on the service from London Bridge To Brighton; these contained three first class trailer cars as well as the Pullman coach but these were downgraded during 1947 and 1948 with the trio being redesignated as '6PUL'. The majority of the '6PUL' stock was withdrawn and scrapped during 1966; some, however, were retained briefly to form new '6COR' units that were designed to be in use temporarily pending the arrival of new stock then under construction. *Charles Firminger/Bob Bridger Collection/Online Transport Archive*

Pictured approaching Burgess Hill is Class H2 No 32424 *Beachy Head.* The eight-coach train is formed of Pullman stock and represents a special organised by the London Branch of the RCTS to mark the centenary of the opening of the LBSCR's Brighton Works. The 'H2' was used on both the Down and Up workings from and to London Victoria. The six locomotives of the 'H2' class were built at Brighton Works; they were based on the earlier 'H1' class designed by Douglas Earle Marsh, who had resigned in July 1911, as modified by his successor Lawson Billinton. All six of the class passed to BR in 1948 but one was withdrawn in May 1949; four of the remaining five survived until withdrawal in 1956. This left No 32424 as the sole survivor; when withdrawn in April 1958, No 32424 had the honour of being the last Atlantic in service on BR. Although none of the class was preserved at the time, in 2000 the Bluebell Railway announced its intention of constructing a replica of No 32424. Work is in progress at the time of writing.
D. Kelk/Online Transport Archive

On 18 July 1959 Class M7 0-4-4T No 30049 stands under the impressive overall roof at Brighton station with a service towards Horsham. The original terminus for the LBSCR at Brighton was designed by David Mocatta and opened in 1841; the Palladian façade of this station is still visible albeit now overshadowed by the later overall roof and the 1883 iron porte cochère. As traffic grew, so the station proved inadequate and was extended initially to accommodate the Brighton, Lewes & Hastings Railway; the three-span overall roof was also completed in 1883, to the design of H. E. Wallis. The whole station is now Grade II* listed. When recorded here, No 30049 was a relatively recent arrival at Brighton shed, having been transferred from Horsham during the five-week period that ended on 18 July 1959; it was transferred to Guildford two years later, from where it was withdrawn in early June 1962. *J. Joyce/Online Transport Archive*

Pictured awaiting departure from Brighton on 3 May 1964 is Class 5BEL No 3052; this was one of the three five-car sets built by Metropolitan Cammell in 1932 for the prestigious 'Southern Belle' – 'Brighton Belle' from June 1934 – Pullman service introduced by the Southern Railway following the electrification of the London to Brighton main line. The three were originally Nos 2051-53, being renumbered 3051-53 in January 1937. Closest to the camera is Driver Motor Brake Parlour Third No 91; the other carriages that comprised No 3052 were two Trailer Parlour Firsts (*Audrey* and

Vera), Trailer Parlour Third (No 87) and a second Driver Motor Brake Parlour Third (No 90). Following the withdrawal of the 'Brighton Belle' service, which last operated on 30 April 1972, all 15 Pullman carriages were sold albeit no five-car set was kept intact. Unfortunately one of the carriages – No 90 from No 3052 – was destroyed by fire in 1991. In 2008 a project to recreate a '5BEL' was launched; the restored unit will include Driver Motor Brake Parlour Third No 91.

John Meredith/Online Transport Archive

The short LBSCR branch to Brighton Kemp Town opened on 2 August 1869. Passenger services over the 1½-mile branch were suspended as a wartime economy measure between 1 January 1917 and 19 August 1919 but were withdrawn entirely by the SR on 31 December 1932. However, occasional specials operated over the route, as on 5 October 1952 when 'Terrier' 0-6-0T No 32636 brought the special organised by the RCTS to mark the centenary of Brighton Works to the line. The two-coach train is seen here awaiting departure with the return working. After the withdrawal of passenger traffic, Kemp Town was retained as a goods yard until final closure came on 14 August 1971. Since closure, the site of the station has been redeveloped as an industrial estate although the southern portal of the tunnel that once provided access to the station remains as a reminder of the railway's presence.
Arthur Davenport/Online Transport Archive

Rowfant station – the only intermediate halt on the East Grinstead Railway when the line opened on 9 July 1855 – served no community other than Rowfant House, the owner of which, Curtis Miranda Lampson, had sold land cheaply to the railway on the provision that a station be provided. This view, taken on 18 May 1963, shows the station from the level crossing immediately to its west. When opened the station was provided with only a single platform; a second platform was added when the loop was installed. The station also possessed a small goods yard. With the development of Gatwick Airport in the 1950s, the yard was used for the storage of aviation fuel; this traffic continued after the station lost its freight facilities on 7 January 1961. The entire line from Three Bridges to Tunbridge Wells was slated for closure in the Beeching Report and services were withdrawn from Three Bridges to Eridge on 2 January 1967. The station building at Rowfant is still extant and much of the trackbed of the former line to East Grinstead is now a footpath, the Worth Way.
Gerald Druce/Online Transport Archive

On 18 May 1963, Class M7 0-4-4T No 30133 awaits departure from Grange Road with the 2.17pm service to East Grinstead. The station opened on 2 April 1860 and served the community of Crawley Down. Until 1865 the station was a request halt and the station was rebuilt, on an enlarged scale, in 1867. Although remaining a single platform, a footbridge adjacent to the signalbox was provided in 1897; although this had disappeared by the date of this photograph. The construction of the station encouraged the development of a number of new country estates and Crawley Down as a community has grown significantly over the years, particularly in the decade after the line's closure. Today the station site has disappeared and been redeveloped as a parade of shops whilst the trackbed through the community has also been lost; to the east and west, however, the route of the line survives as footpaths.

Gerald Druce/Online Transport Archive

As a train for Lewes awaits departure from the Low Level platforms at East Grinstead station, Class H 0-4-4T No 31530 stands at the head of a westbound departure in the High Level platforms on 15 March 1958. Although the branch to East Grinstead remains part of the National Network – and East Grinstead now boasts a rebuilt station (following work completed in 2013) – the High Level platforms were taken out of use following the closure of the line from Eridge to Three Bridges on 2 January 1967 and were subsequently demolished although a replacement footbridge was installed in 1970. The station as seen here represented the third phase of its development and resulted from the opening of the lines from Lewes to East Grinstead and from East Grinstead to Oxted on 1 August 1882 and 10 March 1884 respectively which necessitated the construction of the low level platforms; a connection between the line towards Three Bridges and that towards Oxted was also constructed. Following closure, the trackbed of the Three Bridges route westwards was converted into a footpath; east of the station, however, a section of the disused trackbed was converted into the new A22 which appropriately bears the name 'Beeching Way'.
Gerald Druce/Online Transport Archive

The station at Forest Row – seen here from the west looking towards Ashurst Junction – opened with the line on 1 October 1866. When constructed, it possessed only a single platform but was expanded with a loop and second platform in 1897. Freight traffic was handled in the small goods yard located to the south of the station until facilities were withdrawn on 7 November 1966. During the 1960s, as a result of housing developments around the original village, passenger traffic through Forest Row increased and a number of services that had previously terminated at East Grinstead were extended to serve it. However, this was not sufficient to secure the station and it closed completely with the withdrawal of passenger services on 2 January 1967. The bulk of the station was subsequently demolished. There are, however, some survivors, including the office once occupied by the local coal merchant. The trackbed through Forest Row forms part of the Forest Way footpath although in the immediate vicinity of the station site and to its west the trackbed has been incorporated into an unclassified road.

Denis Cullum courtesy Lens of Sutton Association

Viewed looking towards the east through the arch of the road bridge that carried the B2026 over the line is Hartfield station; the station opened with the line on 1 October 1866 and was closed on 2 January 1967. The station possessed limited freight facilities but these were withdrawn on 7 May 1962. Following the lifting of the track the station building was sold off and is still extant, having been converted into a residence, as is the small goods shed located to the east of the station. The former platform area has been infilled, in order to create a garden, and the Forest Way, which makes use of the former trackbed, deviates slightly to avoid this. *Denis Cullum courtesy Lens of Sutton Association*

Pictured heading west in 1956 with a 6.47pm service from Tunbridge Wells to Victoria heading into Withyham station is an Ivatt-designed 2-6-2T. The station at Withyham opened with the line from East Grinstead to Tunbridge Wells on 1 October 1866. The station was located to the east of a level crossing and was provided with a single platform and a small signalbox, sited behind the photographer, that controlled the crossing. The station closed with the line on 2 January 1967 with the station building being converted into a private house. The trackbed of the line from Ashurst Junction westwards has been converted into a footpath, the Forest Way.
Denis Cullum courtesy Lens of Sutton Association

The first station south from East Grinstead on the Bluebell Line was Kingscote. In May 1962, with the track already rusting, the station has been closed for some seven years when this view looking towards the north was taken. When the legal challenge to the line's original closure in 1955 was made, the plaintiffs relied upon the original Acts that covered the construction of the line and its operation by the LBSCR. These specified only four intermediate stations with both Kingscote – reputed to be the quietest on the entire LBSCR network – and Barcombe excluded when passenger services were restored in 1956. The track between Horsted Keynes and East Grinstead was lifted in 1963 with the station sold and converted into a private house but that was not to be the end of the story. In the 1980s the concept of reconnecting the Bluebell Railway to the BR network developed and, following a public enquiry, planning consent was granted for the work. The Bluebell Railway commenced services to Kingscote in 1994 and this was to be the line's terminus for almost 20 years until the completion of the project to restore the line to East Grinstead in 2013.

Roy Hobbs/Online Transport Archive

The closure of the line from East Grinstead to Lewes was first proposed in 1954; despite local opposition, the last passenger services operated on 29 May 1955 (earlier than planned due to an industrial dispute as the original date was 15 June 1955). However, detailed investigation of the original Acts of 1877 and 1878 relating to the 'Statutory Line' resulted in a court action against BR and, on 7 August 1956, services were restored (calling only at those stations highlighted in the relevant Acts). Pictured approaching West Hoathly from the south on 22 September 1956 with the 3.30pm from Lewes to East Grinstead is Class C2X 0-6-0 No 32438. The reprieve was, however, to be relatively short-lived as, in 1957, BR took the case to the House of Commons. Following a public inquiry, in which BR was censured, the relevant clauses in the Acts were repealed and the line closed again on 17 March 1958.
J. Joyce/Online Transport Archive

The closure of the Lewes to East Grinstead line meant that the only surviving passenger service to Horsted Keynes was the electrified line that ran west to Haywards Heath. However, this route was already threatened with closure – indeed it is recorded in the Beeching Report of March 1963 as one of the lines where closure was proposed – and so there was a relatively brief period, from the reopening of the final part of the Horsted Keynes to Sheffield Park section by the Bluebell Railway in 1962 and the closure of the BR line on 28 October 1963, when trains operated by the preservation society and BR could be seen alongside each other in Horsted Keynes station. On 26 August 1962 whilst ex-SECR Class P 0-6-0T *Primrose* awaits departure with a service towards Sheffield Park, BR Class 2BIL No 2150, one of 36 of the class (Nos 2117-52) constructed in 1938 in connection with the electrification through to Reading, stands in the platform prior to making the 4¾-mile trip to Haywards Heath.
John Meredith/Online Transport Archive

There was only one intermediate station on the line from Haywards Heath to Horsted Keynes; this was at Ardingly, which is pictured here from the west in 1953. The station opened with the line on 3 September 1883 and was primarily constructed the serve the adjacent Ardingly College. Although electrified from 7 July 1935, the branch was already under threat of closure prior to the publication of the Beeching Report and services were withdrawn on 28 October 1963. Subsequently, much of the station was demolished with its site being used as a rail-served stone terminal. The Bluebell Railway owns the trackbed east of Ardingly as has long-term plans to reopen the branch to Copyhold Junction. *Denis Cullum courtesy Lens of Sutton Association*

Known as Fletching & Sheffield Park when first opened on 1 August 1882, the station was renamed as Sheffield Park on 1 January 1883. As an economy measure, the section of line south of Horsted Keynes was completed as a single track although the formation and structures were designed to accommodate double track should the need arise. The station at Sheffield Park was provided with two 400ft long platforms each with a 90ft platform canopy. The main station building was on the Down platform and it is at this platform that Class E4 0-6-0T No 32581 stands with a freight bound for Lewes. Sheffield Park possessed a goods yard; this was situated on the Down side, south of the station, but facilities were withdrawn on 13 June 1955. Although BR had approved closure of the line south of East Grinstead, its actual closure was slightly premature – the last train ran on Saturday 28 May 1955 – as a result of industrial action. Following the legal challenge to the closure, passenger services were restored on 7 August 1956 for a further 18 months. The section from Sheffield Park to Horsted Keynes was preserved following closure by the Bluebell Railway. However the section south from Sheffield Park was closed completely when passenger services over the section were withdrawn for the second time.
John Meredith Collection/Online Transport Archive

The first station south of Sheffield Park en route to Lewes was Newick & Chailey which is viewed from the south on Sunday 16 March 1958 – the day before the station was officially closed but after the last trains had operated. The station had opened on 1 August 1882 when it was provided with substantial buildings on both the Up and Down platforms with a footbridge linking the two. However, the building on the Up platform and the footbridge were demolished in the 1930s (although evidence of the lost footbridge is evident on the surviving station building on the Down side). The East Grinstead to Lewes line was initially closed on 28 May 1955, with freight facilities being withdrawn from Newick & Chailey on 13 June 1955, and it was a resident of Chailey – Margery Bessemer – who instituted the legal action that resulted in BR reluctantly restoring a passenger service on 7 August 1956 pending the passing of new legislation to facilitate closure again. With powers in place, the line was closed for a second time officially on 17 March 1958 with the section south of Sheffield Park being lifted two years later. The station was demolished in the late 1960s and much of the site infilled prior to redevelopment for housing. *Charles Firminger/Bob Bridger Collection/Online Transport Archive*

Originally known as New Barcombe when opened on 1 August 1882, the station at Barcombe is pictured here looking towards the north. There was a small goods yard to the north of the station; freight facilities were handled at the station until 13 June 1955 when the line from East Grinstead to Lewes was officially closed. However, as a result of a strike involving ASLEF, the final passenger service operated on 28 May 1955. Although the closure of the line was successfully contested as it was counter to the original Acts of Parliament that sanctioned the line, with services being reintroduced on 7 August 1956, the station at Barcombe was not reopened. BR services from East Grinstead to Lewes were finally withdrawn on 17 March 1958. The station building at Barcombe is still extant, having been converted into a private house. *Marcus Eavis/Online Transport Archive*

Pictured approaching Cooksbridge station on 14 August 1955 with the Up boat train from Newhaven is the first of the trio of the ex-SR electric locomotives – No 20001 – in the predominantly black livery then worn by the locomotives. Built as No CC1 at Ashford Works during 1940 and 1941, as the first of the future BR Class 70, No 20001 was designed by Oliver Bullied, the SR's Chief Mechanical Engineer, and Alfred Raworth, the Chief Electrical Engineer. In producing a locomotive capable of operating over the third-rail network, the design had to be capable of maintaining power when the locomotive passed over gaps in the conductor rail. This was achieved by a combination of motor generators and flywheels known as boosters, after which the class was nicknamed. A second locomotive – No CC2 – was completed at Ashford Works during 1945 with a third, with modifications, being completed by BR at Brighton Works in 1948. The three locomotives were associated with the Newhaven boat trains for much of their career but were withdrawn, as non-standard between October 1968 and January 1969. Although none carried the BR TOPS number, No 20001 did end up in BR Rail Blue livery. Cooksbridge station – known originally as Cook's Bridge until renamed in 1885 – opened with the line from Wivelsfield to Lewes on 1 October 1847. *R. C. Riley/Transport Treasury*

On 22 September 1956 Class C2X 0-6-0 No 32442 awaits departure from Lewes with the 11.30am service to East Grinstead. Although the first station in Lewes opened in June 1846, the station illustrated here was the result of the relocation of the station in November 1857 and its substantial rebuilding three decades later; the rebuilt station opened on 27 June 1889. The 'C2X class represented a rebuild, undertaken by Lawson Billinton, of the earlier 'C' class designed by Earle Marsh; a total of 45 locomotives were modified between 1908 and 1940 with increased diameter boilers and extended smokeboxes. No 32442 was originally completed at Vulcan Foundry in May 1893; when recorded here, the locomotive was allocated to Brighton shed from where it was withdrawn in early 1960.
Marcus Eavis/Online Transport Archive

Viewed amidst an impressive array of semaphore signals at the east end of Lewes station Class 4CIG (later Class 421) No 7309 approaches the station with an Up service from Hastings to Victoria on 10 June 1966. The initial batch of the EMU, Nos 7301-36, was constructed at the Holgate Road, York, carriage works between 1963 and 1966 for use primarily on services on the Brighton line; a second batch, Nos 7337-438 (also constructed at York), were delivered between 1970 and 1972 for use on the Portsmouth line.

John Meredith/Online Transport Archive

Following the opening of its line to Newhaven, the LBSCR developed the harbour and provided a number of quayside lines to service this. One of these was West Quay, where the sidings were linked to the main line via a tramway included in the road bridge over the River Ouse. Pictured crossing the bridge from West Quay to the main line in May 1962 is 'Terrier' 0-6-0T No 32670; by this date, the line was approaching the end as it closed on 10 August 1962 when sister locomotive No 32678 was employed to clear all remaining wagons from the yard. No 32670 was last overhauled in 1960, some 88 years after it had been built in 1872, and was withdrawn following the closure of the Hayling Island branch in late 1963. Subsequently preserved, the locomotive is now back at an earlier home – the Kent & East Sussex Railway – and is, at the time of writing, undergoing a major overhaul.
Roy Hobbs/Online Transport Archive

Viewed from the branch that once provided access to the quay at Newhaven, Class HA (later Class 71) No E5002 is seen entering Newhaven Harbour station light engine on 17 July 1965. The future Harbour station was opened on 8 December 1847 as Newhaven Wharf for Paris and became known as Newhaven Harbour in 1884. Its terminal platforms were replaced two years later by the station that was ultimately known as Newhaven Marine with the through platforms serving the line to Seaford following its opening on 1 June 1864. A total of 24 of Class HA Bo-Bo electric locomotives were constructed at Doncaster Works, entering service between December 1959 and November 1960. However, as work declined a number were placed into store and, in order to extend their operational range, 10 of the class were converted into electro-diesels during 1968 (being reclassified as Class HB – later Class 74). The remaining 12 locomotives were withdrawn en masse in November 1977 when their duties were taken over by Class 33s; one of the type – No 71001 (ex-E5001) – was preserved as part of the National Collection.
John Meredith/Online Transport Archive

On 8 April 1962 Bulleid-designed Class Q1 0-6-0 No 33028 is seen awaiting departure from Ashurst station with the 6.8pm southbound service. The line from Hurst Green Junction to Ashurst Junction, south of the station, was a relatively late addition to the local network, being opened to Edenbridge on 2 January 1888 and thence through to Ashurst Junction on the following 1 October. Ashurst station opened with the line; the suffix 'Kent' was added to the station name on 21 September 1996 in order to differentiate it from the station in the New Forest. The station now provides a loop on the otherwise single-track section of the Uckfield branch between Hever and Crowborough. *James Harrold/Transport Treasury*

On 22 April 1961 Class U1 2-6-0 No 31893 enters Eridge station with an Up service. The station opened, courtesy of the LBSCR-backed Brighton, Uckfield & Tunbridge Wells Railway, on 3 August 1868. In addition to the services on the line from Oxted through Uckfield to Lewes, the station was also used by services on the lines east to Tunbridge Wells and south-east towards Eastbourne via Hailsham until these were closed on 6 July 1985 and 14 June 1965 respectively. Following the singling of the Uckfield line in 1990, BR services were restricted to the former Up platform with the Down platform redundant. However, preservation – courtesy of the Spa Valley Railway – of the line from Eridge to Tunbridge Wells West, resulted in the restoration of the Down island platform with services bring reintroduced over the preserved line to Eridge on 25 March 2011. *Dave Clark/The Transport Library*

On an unknown date during 1958, Class U1 2-6-0 No 31910 is seen approaching Crowborough & Jarvis Brook from the north with the 4.49pm Down service from Victoria to Brighton. The station opened as Rotherfield on 3 August 1868, before being renamed Crowfield on 1 August 1880 following the opening of the line from Eridge to Hailsham. It became Crowborough & Jarvis Brook on 1 May 1897 before reverting to Crowborough on 12 May 1980. The station is still open and is now at the northern end of a short section of double track that extends southwards through Crowborough Tunnel to Greenhurst.
Denis Cullum courtesy Lens of Sutton Association

Pictured arriving at Uckfield station during 1958 with a 1.10pm service from Tonbridge to Brighton is BR Standard 2-6-4T No 80032. The railway first reached Uckfield from the south, courtesy of the Lewes & Uckfield Railway, on 11 October 1858. It was to be a further decade before the line was extended northwards to Groombridge; this opened to freight during 1867 and to passenger traffic on 3 August 1868. Although the entire line from Eridge to Lewes was scheduled for closure in the Beeching Report, the section from Uckfield to Eridge was reprieved with the line south from Uckfield closing on 24 February

1969. The original station was closed on 13 May 1991 when a new station, located east of the level crossing, was opened; although the original building was initially left intact, it suffered from flood damage and was demolished in late 2000. The Uckfield branch, which remains diesel operated, has been singled. One survivor from this 1958 view is the Saxby & Farmer signalbox, which once controlled the High Street crossing, that is now preserved in the ownership of Uckfield Town Council.
Denis Cullum courtesy Lens of Sutton Association

The first station south of Eridge on the line towards Polegate on the Cuckoo line was Rotherfield & Mark Cross. Rotherfield had originally been served by a station on the route to Uckfield but the original station was renamed Crowborough when this station was opened with the line to Hailsham on 1 September 1880. The station was opened as simply Rotherfield; it gained the '& Mark Cross' suffix on 1 November 1901. Pictured entering the station on 19 April 1965 from the north are a pair of DEMUs with Class

207 No 1319 leading. This was the last of the class to enter service – in August 1962. The 'East Sussex' units were used on the Cuckoo and the Three Bridges to Tunbridge Wells routes until their closure; thereafter the units were transferred to other services. Rotherfield & Mark Cross lost its freight facilities on 8 October 1962 and was to close completely with the line on 14 June 1965. *A. M. Logan/Online Transport Archive*

It is 11 June 1965 and the story of the Cuckoo Line is soon to be completed as a BR Standard 2-6-4T stands in the station at Rotherfield & Mark Cross with a southbound service. Since closure the station house and main station building have both been converted into private houses; the attractive signalbox visible in this 11965 view has, however, been demolished although the nameboard is now affixed to one of the houses. The goods shed – freight facilities were withdrawn on 8 October 1962 – has been demolished and the site of the shed and yard has been utilised for housing. *A. M. Logan/Online Transport Archive*

On 1 June 1957 BR Standard 2-6-4T No 80147 approaches Mayfield station from the south with a service heading towards Eridge. The station, which was located to the west of the community it served, was opened with the 9¾-mile section north from Heathfield. In addition to the goods yard, which survived until 6 May 1963 (the site of which was subsequently redeveloped for housing), there was also until 1950 a private siding that served the local milk depot. Although the main station building, situated on the Down platform, is still extant and is now a private residence, the construction of the A267 Mayfield bypass resulted in the loss of the remains of the Up platform and the trackbed, with the result that the surviving structure now stands at some height above the new road, which opened in 1991.
Peter Hay/Transport Treasury

Heathfield station was approached from the north through a short – 265-yard long – tunnel, the southern portal of which is visible in the background on 19 April 1958 as BR Standard 2-6-4T No 80151 stands in the station with a southbound service. The station opened on 3 April 1880 when the line from Hailsham was opened; the section from Heathfield to Eridge opened on 1 September 1880. Passenger services ceased on 14 June 1965 between Hailsham and Eridge when the section north of Heathfield closed completely. Freight facilities were retained at Heathfield until 26 April 1968 when, following damage to a bridge which was deemed uneconomic to repair, the line was closed completely north of Hailsham. Since closure, the station site has been cleared and redeveloped as an industrial estate although the trackbed south to Polegate survives as the Cuckoo Trail. Heathfeld Tunnel was restored in the early 21st century as part of a northern extension to the trail but, although reopened, it was subsequently closed following issues of crime and antisocial behaviour. The station house also survives as a private residence whilst the road level booking office is extant, having been converted into a shop and café. *Neville Stead Collection/Transport Treasury*

On 1 June 1957 BR Standard 2-6-4T No 80154 is pictured arriving at Horam station with a southbound service towards Polegate and Eastbourne. Opened originally as Horam Road for Waldon on 3 April 1880, the station underwent various renamings before the name was settled as Horam on 21 September 1953. The station was one of the key sources of freight traffic on the line as it was the location of Express Dairy's main depot. However, freight facilities were withdrawn from the station on 6 May 1963. Following the line's closure to passenger traffic, freight trains continued to operate through Horam until the complete closure of the section from Hailsham to Heathfield on 26 April 1968. At that date the station buildings were still substantially complete but the shelter on the Down platform was demolished by the early 1970s and the main station on the Up platform followed in the early 1990s when much of the site was redeveloped for housing. There are, however, still remnants of the platforms and the trackbed through the station has been incorporated into part of the Cuckoo Trail. *Peter Hay/Transport Treasury*

Viewed looking towards the north on 28 October 1950, ex-LMS 2-6-4T No 42101 is seen entering the station at Hellingly with a service from Tunbridge Wells West to Eastbourne. The station was on the section of the 'Cuckoo' line from Hailsham to Heathfield that opened on 3 April 1880. Apart from the single platform, Hellingly also possessed a small goods yard to the south of the station; freight facilities were withdrawn on 28 September 1964. The overhead visible to the right of the train was used by the privately-owned line that provided a link from the station Hellingly Mental Hospital. Until 1932 there was a small wooden platform located on the east side of the running line for use by passengers making use of the line to the hospital. The section of the 'Cuckoo' line from Hailsham to Heathfield, retained for freight traffic after the line's closure to passenger traffic, closed completely on 26 April 1968. Today, Hellingly is still intact, having been converted into a private residence, with the trackbed through the station having been converted into part of the Cuckoo Trail footpath.
John Meredith/Online Transport Archive

In 1899, following East Sussex County Council's purchase of 400 acres to the east of Hellingly in order to construct a new asylum (later known as Hellingly Hospital), a standard gauge line from Hellingly to the new hospital was constructed. Extending for 1¼ miles, the line was initially operated by steam but, in 1902, the route was electrified and a single 0-4-0 locomotives provided by Robert W. Blackwell & Co was supplied. The origins of the locomotive – pictured here at Hellingly station on 23 May 1954 – are uncertain and it may have been imported from Germany by the supplier. Passenger services were introduced to the line on 20 July 1903 – the same day that the new hospital opened. After World War 1 passenger traffic declined and ceased completely – except for specials – in 1932; thereafter, the line remained open to transport coal to the hospital. This traffic ceased on 10 March 1959, following the decision to convert the hospital's boilers to oil firing, and the line closed officially on 25 March 1959 following the removal of the final wagons although a few specials operated after that date. The track and overhead were dismantled in the early 1960s.

John Meredith/Online Transport Archive

On 5 September 1961 Class U1 2-6-0 No 31892 is recorded running round its train at Hailsham prior to departing with the 6pm service to Hailsham. The station originally opened as the terminus of the LBSCR branch from Polegate on 15 May 1849; it was not until 5 April 1880 that the line was extended northwards to Heathfield. Apart from the two platform station, which remained the terminus some services from Eastbourne (as in the instance illustrated here), Hailsham also boasted a large goods shed that was situated to the south of the passenger station. Although passenger traffic between Hailsham and Eridge ceased on 14 June 1965, services continued to serve the Polegate to Hailsham section until 9 September 1968. Freight traffic between Hailsham and Heathfield had ceased in April 1968 and, with freight facilities having been withdrawn from Hailsham on 5 August 1968, the end of passenger services resulted in the closure of the last section of the Cuckoo line. The track north from Polegate was lifted in 1969. Apart from the goods shed, which was derelict by 1975, the station buildings had been demolished by the mid-1970s and the surviving platform sections and goods shed were cleared by the early 1980s as the site was redeveloped for housing. North of the road overbridge situated immediately to the north of the station, the trackbed survives and represents the southern section of the Cuckoo Trail.
James Harrold/Transport Treasury

Class 205 DEMU No 1116 departs from Polegate station on 10 June 1966 with a service from Hailsham to Eastbourne. The train is passing Polegate B (or East) box as to heads towards its ultimate destination. Although there was originally a triangular junction to the east of Polegate station, with a direct line towards Stone Cross Junction providing a route that bypassed Eastbourne, the direct line was increasingly little used and was officially closed on 6 January 1969 although was still used by engineering trains until 8 September 1974 when the junction at Polegate B was severed. Latterly numbered 205016, this unit was finally withdrawn after 37 years of service in August 1994 and subsequently scrapped. *John Meredith/Online Transport Archive*

With the unofficial name 'Sir George Terry' chalked on its smokebox, BR Standard 2-6-4T No 80145 is seen running around its train at Eastbourne on 8 June 1965. The station at Eastbourne was relocated to the current site in 1872 as a result of the increased number of services to and from the resort. The station, which is now Grade II listed, was rebuilt in 1886 to the designs of Frederick Dale Banister, the LBSCR's Chief Engineer between 1860 and 1896. When recorded here No 80145, which had been completed at Brighton Works in October 1956, was coming to the end of an 18-month period allocated to Redhill; it was transferred to Salisbury following the closure of the Cuckoo line, where it was stored until a final transfer saw it move to Nine Elms in early 1966 from where it was withdrawn in June 1967.

A. M. Logan/Online Transport Archive

On 14 August 1955 Class U1 2-6-0 No 31907 is seen heading south from Frant with a ramblers' special. The South Eastern Railway line from Tonbridge to a temporary station at Tunbridge Wells opened on 20 September 1845 and was extended to a permanent station in the town – know as Tunbridge Wells Central between 9 July 1923 and 14 May 1979 – on 25 November 1846. The line was extended through Frant to Robertsbridge on 1 September 1851 and the station at Frant opened with the line. It has a main building – now Grade II listed – designed by William Tress. The 21-strong 'U1' class – BR Nos 31890-910 – owed their origins to the rebuilding at Ashford of the sole Class K1 2-6-4T as a 2-6-0 following the Sevenoaks accident of 25 August 1927. The remaining 20 locomotives were all built at Eastleigh between June and November 1931. All of the class remained in service at the start of 1962 but, by the end of that year, all bar four had been withdrawn; the final example – appropriately No 31910 – was withdrawn in July 1963.

R. C. Riley/Transport Treasury

In April 1957 Class V 'Schools' No 30903 *Dulwich* is seen from the Up platform at Wadhurst as it heads south with a service towards Hastings. The station at Wadhurst opened with the line through to Robertsbridge on 1 September 1851. When recorded here the 'Schools' was approaching the end of its career on the Hastings line; having been based at St Leonards throughout the period since Nationalisation, No 30903 was transferred to Nine Elms by mid-June 1957. It was to spend a year based there before a final transfer saw the locomotive reallocated to Basingstoke from where it was withdrawn in early December 1961.
Peter Hay/Transport Treasury

On 27 April 1957 'Schools' class 4-4-0 No 30924 *Haileybury* heads a Down service into Stonegate station. The SER line from Tunbridge Wells southwards was authorised in 1846 with the section between there and Robertsbridge opening on 1 September 1851. Stonegate station opened on the same day; it was known originally as Witherenden until December 1851 when it was renamed Ticehurst Road. It retained that name until 16 June 1847 when it was renamed Stonegate. Designed by Richard Maunsell, the 40-strong 'Schools' class was the last type of 4-4-0 produced for any railway in Britain and represented the most powerful 4-4-0 design in Europe. Designed to have a high route availability, the cab sides were sloped inwards in order to provide clearance to work the more restricted loading gauge of the Tunbridge Wells to Hastings line. All of the type remained in service until the end of 1960 but modernisation of the routes over which they operated resulted in the final examples being withdrawn by the end of 1962. Three examples of the class – Nos 30925 *Cheltenham*, 30926 *Repton* and 30928 *Stowe* – survive in preservation.
Peter Hay/Transport Treasury

On 26 March 1956 Class L 4-4-0 No 31767 has just passed through Etchingham station as it heads north with the 2.35pm service from Hastings to Tonbridge. In 1913 Henry Wainwright retired as Locomotive, Carriage & Wagon Superintendent of the South Eastern & Chatham Railway; just before he retired, he designed a new class of 4-4-0 but it was left to his successor – Richard Maunsell – to complete the work and a total of 22 locomotives were built during 1914. Of these 12 – later BR Nos 31760-71 – were constructed by Beyer Peacock with the remainder – BR Nos 31772-81 – being completed by A. Borsig of Berlin; fortunately the latter, which were nicknamed 'Germans', were all delivered before the German army invaded Belgium, thus triggering the start of World War 1. All 22 of the class survived until the mid-1950s, with the first withdrawal occurring in December 1956. All had been withdrawn by the end of 1961; No 31767 succumbed relatively early, in October 1958.

Julian Thompson/Online Transport Archive

Pictured awaiting departure from the Kent & East Sussex platform at Robertsbridge station is another of the 'Terrier' class 0-6-0Ts – probably No 32659. Built at Brighton as LBSCR No 59 *Cheam* in October 1875, the locomotive was rebuilt from 'A1' to 'A1X' in December 1921. When recorded here, No 32659 was approaching the end of its main-line career, being withdrawn from Ashford shed in August 1953. This was not to be the end of the locomotive's career, however, as it was transferred to departmental stock and renumbered DS681. Allocated to Lancing Carriage Works, it remained in departmental use until June 1963 when it was taken out of service. The locomotive was scrapped at Eastleigh later the same month. The preserved Rother Valley Railway, which was first established in 1991 with the aim of restoring the line to link up with the preserved Kent & East Sussex at Bodiam, is based at Robertsbridge and a section of line towards Northbridge Street has been relayed as has a connection into the National Network. At the time of writing, a decision is awaited from the public enquiry held on the railway's plans for the reopening of the line from Northbridge Street to Junction Road (the current railhead for the preserved Kent & East Sussex).

Neil Davenport/Online Transport Archive

It is 19 June 1948 but, more than six months after the Nationalisation of the railways, Kent & East Sussex 'Terrier' No 3 still proudly carries its pre-Nationalisation as it approaches Robertsbridge station. No 3 was one of a number of the ex-LBSCR class to be owned by the Kent & East Sussex. Originally built at Brighton Works in 1872 as LBSCR No 70 *Poplar*, the locomotive was purchased for the Kent & East Sussex in 1901. Withdrawn in 1931, the locomotive was restored to service two years later using parts from sister locomotive No 5 *Rolvenden* – which had originally been LBSCR No 71 *Wapping* – that was scrapped in 1938. Modified into an 'A1X' with a new boiler and extended firebox in 1943, the locomotive passed to BR in 1948 and became No 32670. Withdrawn in November 1963, it was subsequently preserved and is now, appropriately, based on the preserved Kent & East Sussex. *John Meredith/Online Transport Archive*

The first intermediate station on the Kent & East Sussex line after departing from Robertsbridge was Salehurst Halt, which is pictured here on 29 November 1953, less than two months before passenger services were withdrawn. The halt first appeared in the public timetable on 23 September 1929 but it had existed – untimetabled – for more than a quarter of a century prior to that date. The driving force for the construction of the simple station – completion of which was notified to the Board of Trade by Col Holman F. Stephens in July 1903 – was the vicar of Salehurst, the Rev Edward Sing, who was keen that trains could stop so that the church organist, who lived in Bodiam, could reach the church for services on Wednesdays and Sundays if the weather was bad and precluded the use of her car. Following the line's closure in January 1954, the platform was demolished.
Neville Stead Collection/Transport Treasury

Heading east from Salehurst Halt, the next station was Junction Road Halt (or Junction Road for Hawkhurst), which is pictured here on 1 November 1953 as a mother and child await the arrival of a Robertsbridge-bound train behind 'Terrier' No 32678 on 1 November 1953. The origins of the halt lay in a platform erected in 1900 and listed for use in *Bradshaw* briefly between January and May 1901 and again from June 1903 after the existence of the station had been discovered by the Board of Trade inspector Maj John Wallace Pringle during an official inspection of the line. Limited freight facilities were added to the west of the station in 1909 and the station was officially known as a Halt from 1939.

Regular passenger services ceased in January 1954 although the platform was used by hop picker specials until the late 1950s – the site was close to the Guinness brewery's hop farm. Freight traffic continued until 12 June 1961. Following closure of the line, the track was lifted but on 28 March 2011 the section of line westwards to Junction Road was formally reopened as part of the extended preserved Kent & East Sussex Railway. Although services operated by the K&ESR travel to and from Junction Road, there is no station and passengers cannot board or leave the train. The long-term aspiration is for the line to be restored through to Robertsbridge. *Neville Stead Collection/Transport Treasury*

Pictured awaiting departure from Bodiam station with a westbound service towards Robertsbridge on 18 April 1953 is one of the 'Terrier' class 0-6-0Ts with which the Kent & East Sussex line was synonymous in its later years. The station at Bodiam opened on 2 April 1900. A siding, which also acted as a passing loop, was added a decade later. The station was surrounded by hop fields, many of which were owned by the brewers Guinness, and the line carried many hop-pickers during the season. By the date that this photograph was taken, the line's fortunes were in decline; passenger services from Robertsbridge to Headcorn were withdrawn on 4 January 1954, on which date the line north of Tenterden Town closed completely. The line closed completely from Hodson's Siding in Robertsbridge to Tenterden Town on 12 June 1961 although the section from Tenterden Town to Bodiam was subsequently acquired for preservation. The line from Northiam to Bodiam reopened in 2000 and the track currently extends a further mile westwards to the site of Junction Road station. *Neil Davenport/Online Transport Archive*

Pictured heading from Mountfield Tunnel during 1954 with a service from Charing Cross to Hastings is 'Schools' class 4-4-0 No 30926 *Repton* – which was preserved following withdrawal in December 1962 and is now based on the North Yorkshire Moors Railway after having spent much of its earlier career in preservation in North America. Shortly after the completion of the SER's main line to Hastings, problems appeared with a number of tunnels following investigation when there was a partial collapse in Mountfield Tunnel during 1855. The poor quality of the workmanship resulted in the necessity for remedial work that restricted the loading gauge through the affected tunnels. In the late 1930s further work was required to underpin Mountfield Tunnel whilst a further partial collapse on 17 November 1974 led to the track being singled through the structure.
Denis Cullum courtesy Lens of Sutton Association

Mountfield Halt – viewed here from the south in 1954 – was situated just to the south of the tunnel. The station, with its platforms constructed from sleepers, first appeared in *Bradshaw* in September 1923. Losing its suffix on 5 May 1969, the station was closed on 6 October the same year. Although long closed, traces of the station are still extant. Between the station and the tunnel are the sidings associated with the British Gypsum quarry. *Denis Cullum courtesy Lens of Sutton Association*

On 14 September 1953, Ashford-allocated Class L No 31774 approaches the Down platform at Battle with the 3.28pm service from Tonbridge to Hastings. The station opened on 1 January 1852 with its buildings designed by William Tress in the Gothic Revival style. The buildings – which are influenced by the proximity of the station to the remains of the massive monastery built to commemorate the Battle of Hasting – are regarded as amongst the finest Gothic Revival stations in the country and are now Grade II listed. The staggered platforms did not originally overlap but do so now as a result of extensions to accommodate eight-coach trains after electrification in 1986. In 1913, just before he retired, Harry Wainwright designed a larger class of 4-4-0 than the existing Class D; the new 'L' class was slightly modified by his successor, Richard Maunsell, before a total of 22 were produced during 1914. Of these, 12 were constructed by Beyer Peacock in Manchester but the remaining 10 – eventually BR Nos 31772-81 – were constructed by Borsig in Germany. Being delivered in July 1914, these entered service just before the outbreak of World War 1 and became nicknamed 'Germans'. All were withdrawn between 1956 and the end of 1961, with No 31774 succumbing in December 1958 – the first of the 'Germans' to be withdrawn.
D. Kelk/Online Transport Archive

The junction for the short branch to Bexhill West was at Crowhurst and on 30 May 1958 the Push-Pull service is pictured in the Down bay platform at Crowhurst. Although the final connection in the SER's line from Tunbridge Wells to Hastings – the section from Battle to Bopeep Junction – was opened on 1 February 1852 no station was provided at Crowhurst until five decades later when, on 1 June 1902, it was opened with the branch. The station was provided with two through platforms with bays at the southern end of each to accommodate the branch line services. The bay platforms continued in use until 15 June 1964. The branch service operated into the bay on the Up (northbound) platform to connect with Up services; once the latter had departed, the stock was shunted into the Down platform – as seen here – to await the arrival of the next Down service. Visible in the distance is one of the two signalboxes – Crowhurst No 2 – that controlled the station; Crowhurst No 1 was located to the north of the station. The bulk of the station buildings were demolished in the mid-1980s. *Bernard Harrison/Bob Bridge Collection/Online Transport Archive*

There was only one intermediate station on the branch between Crowhurst and Bexhill West; this was situated at Sidley where Class H 0-4-4T No 31161 is pictured on 3 June 1958. The station was situated in a cutting with the main station buildings sited at street level. A small goods yard was served; this was located to the west of the station and can in the background of this view. Freight facilities were withdrawn on 9 September 1963. Following closure to passenger traffic in June 1964 the track was lifted the following year and the platform buildings and platforms demolished. The street level booking office was demolished in 1971 with the site being occupied by a new petrol filling station. The ex-goods shed, which had been sold for commercial use in the late 1920s, survived in an increasingly derelict condition until its was demolished in 2009. The trackbed through Sidley was redeveloped about a decade ago and now forms the route of the A2690 Combe Valley Way. *Terry Gough/The Transport Library*

On 23 June 1952 Class D3 0-4-4T No 32390 awaits departure from Bexhill West with a service towards Crowhurst. Bexhill West was the terminus of the 4½-mile branch that was promoted by the South Eastern Railway supported Crowhurst, Sidley & Bexhill Railway that was authorised on 15 July 1897 and opened on 1 June 1902. The line was operated from opening by the SER and formally vested in the larger railway in January 1907. Services were suspended as a wartime measure between 1 January 1917 until 1 March 1919. Freight facilities were withdrawn from the station on 9 September 1963 and the line closed completely with the withdrawal of passenger services on 15 June 1964. The substantial station at the terminus, which survives and is now Grade II listed, was designed for the railway by Charles S. Barry, the son of Sir Charles Barry (the architect along with Pugin of the rebuilt Palace of Westminster), and C. E. Mercer. The station was provided with two 700ft-long island platforms; only one of the island platforms was provided with a canopy; this served platforms 1 and 2. The second island platform – serving platform 3 (platform 4 never received track) – was little used.

Neville Stead Collection/Transport Treasury

Located just to the west of Bexhill, the station at Collington – seen here on 14 August 1956 as Class 4LAV No 2950 approaches from the west – was opened as Collington Wood Halt on 11 September 1905. However, it closed a year later on 1 September 1906 before reopening as West Bexhill Halt on 1 June 1911. Renamed Collington Halt on 1 November 1929, the suffix was dropped on 5 May 1969. A total of 35 '4LAV' units were constructed – 33 between 1930 and 1932 with the remaining two being completed during 1939 and 1940 – at Eastleigh for use on semi-fast services between London and the Sussex coast. The initial batch was originally numbered 1921-53 becoming Nos 2921-53 as part of the SR renumbering in early 1937. Withdrawal of the majority of the class took place during 1968 with the final examples succumbing in April 1969. *Terry Gough/The Transport Library*

Bexhill Central station – the suffix was carried from 9 July 1923 until the late 1960s and after the closure of Bexhill West – was the result of a major rebuilding that was completed in June 1902; the main station building is now Grade II listed. Seen approaching Bexhill Central box, which was installed by Saxby & Farmer in 1876 and which is still extant, with an eastbound freight on 31 May 1962 is 'K' class 2-6-0 No 32339. Designed by Lawson Billinton, the first of the 17-strong class – BR Nos 32337-53 – was completed at Brighton in 1913. The first 10 were completed between then and 1916 with the remaining seven following between December 1920 and March 1921; plans to construct a further three were cancelled by the newly created SR. The type, designed for both passenger and freight work, was the most powerful produced for the LBSCR and did sterling work during both World Wars. All 17 remained in service until 1962 but were all withdrawn during November and December that year although the harsh winter of 1962/63 resulted in at least one being given a temporary reprieve. The nascent Bluebell Railway hoped to preserve an example; however, the pressure of fundraising for the purchase of the line meant that this proved a project too far and all 17 were scrapped by the end of October 1964.

Neville Stead Collection/Transport Treasury

On 27 March 1956 an unidentified 'Schools' class 4-4-0 approaches West St Leonards with a Down service from Charing Cross to Hastings. Although the line from Robertsbridge to St Leonards opened in February 1852 it was not until 1 October 1887 that the station at West St Leonards opened.
J. Joyce/Online Transport Archive

Viewed towards the east, an unidentified 'Schools' class 4-4-0 is seen departing from Hasting station with an Up service towards Tunbridge Wells and London. The station at Hastings was originally shared – not wholly amicably – between the London, Brighton & South Coast and South Eastern railways. The station opened on 13 February 1851 with the opening – courtesy of the Brighton, Lewes & Hastings Railway – of the final section from St Leonards through to Hastings and of the SER line from Ashford. The final link in the local network came with the opening of the line from Robertsbridge on 1 February 1852. The original station was 'V' shaped and comprised two elements – a terminus for services to and from Brighton with through platforms for the SER services – but the station as illustrated here was the product of a major rebuilding in the 1930s when island platforms were constructed. The station buildings were reconstructed in a neo-Georgian style by the SR's then Chief Architect, James Robb Scott. The main station building was itself demolished to be replaced by a new structure in 2004.
J. Joyce/Online Transport Archive

Pictured approaching the westbound platform at Rye is a Class L 4-4-0 in September 1954. Although the first train reached the station on 28 October 1850 it was not until 13 February 1851 that the station – along with the SER line from Ashford to Hastings – was opened. The main station buildings, situated behind the photographer, were designed by William Tress and are now Grade II listed as is the signalbox of 1894. Also still extant is the platform shelter visible on the eastbound platform. Freight traffic continued to be handled until facilities were withdrawn on 9 September 1963. Slightly to the west of the station, a one-mile branch provided a connection to Rye harbour; this was opened in 1854 and finally closed on 29 January 1960, although it was little used in later years.

Alec Ford/Transport Treasury